Thor "Bushman" Ollie Janson
GUATEMALA

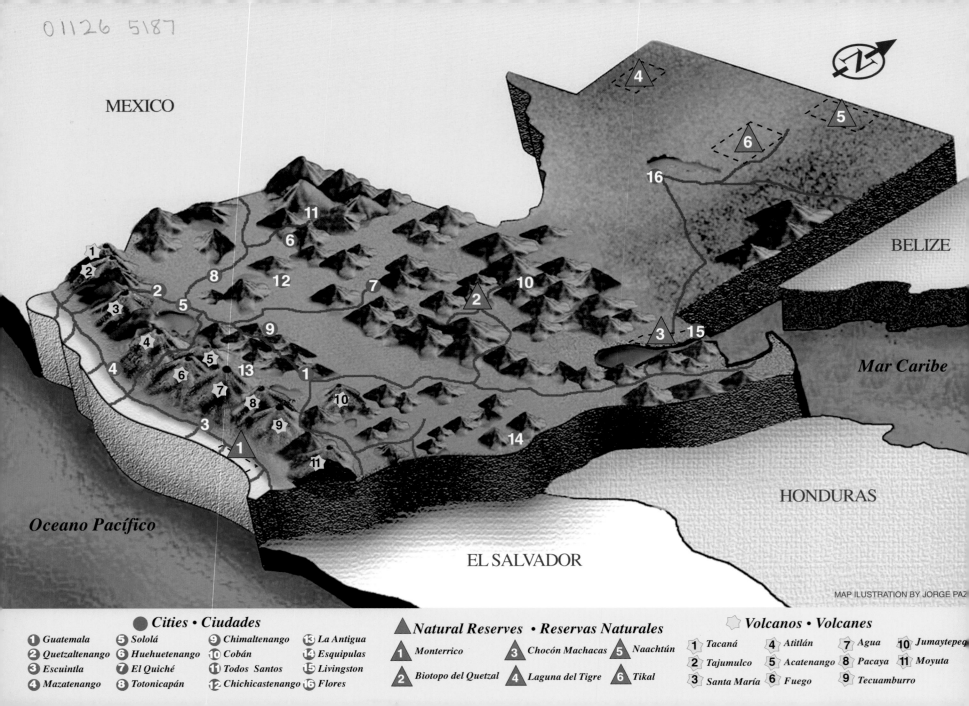

01126 5187

MEXICO

BELIZE

Mar Caribe

HONDURAS

Oceano Pacífico

EL SALVADOR

● Cities • Ciudades

1 Guatemala
2 Quetzaltenango
3 Escuintla
4 Mazatenango
5 Sololá
6 Huehuetenango
7 El Quiché
8 Totonicapán
9 Chimaltenango
10 Cobán
11 Todos Santos
12 Chichicastenango
13 La Antigua
14 Esquipulas
15 Livingston
16 Flores

▲ Natural Reserves • Reservas Naturales

1 Monterrico
2 Biotopo del Quetzal
3 Chocón Machacas
4 Laguna del Tigre
5 Naachtún
6 Tikal

⬡ Volcanos • Volcanes

1 Tacaná
2 Tajumulco
3 Santa María
4 Atitlán
5 Acatenango
6 Fuego
7 Agua
8 Pacaya
9 Tecuamburro
10 Jumaytepeq
11 Moyuta

CONTENTS

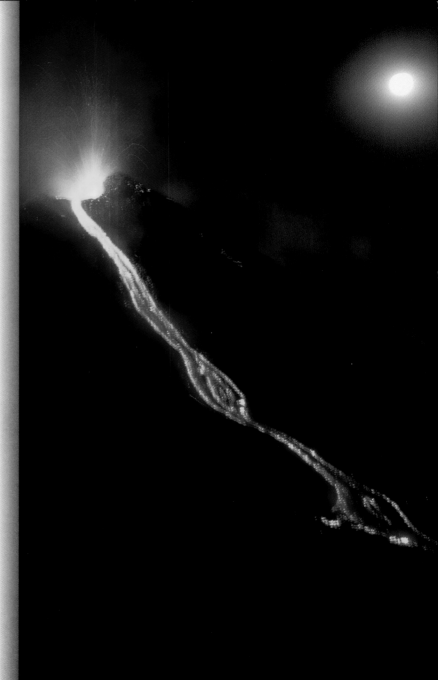

During my explorations of Mayan America I have noticed that the indigenous people of this region exhibit a very wide range of physical traits. The Maya of the northern lowlands are rather short and stout with large round heads and look approximately the same as the images we see depicted in the paintings on Classic Period ceramics from Tikal. The highland Mayan tribes have a decidedly different appearance. I have seen residents from Todos Santos Cuchumatán who look straight out of a photo from Tibet. I have seen faces from the central highlands which make me feel like I am back in a market in Cambodia. I have been struck by the similarity between beautiful Mayan women and friends who are from Polynesia. Even the local residents in Guatemala refer to some of their fellow natives as *chinita* or *chinito* because of their pronounced Chinese appearance. These facts, among others, have led me to speculate for many years that the early colonists of Central America did not all arrive in a single wave of migration out of Asia, over the Bering Land Bridge and then southward. I believe that it is more probable that the colonization of Guatemala was the result of numerous arrivals of people of different origins; some by land and others by sea. Knowledge about the early movements of humans around the planet is still a *terra incognita* to scholars but further archaeological investigation should reveal a picture quite different than we find today in our university text books.

The first solid evidence for a human presence in Guatemala dates from around 10,000 B.C. and is comprised of human remains in association with primitive tools and the remains of mastodon and deer. It is thought that these were early hunters who arrived in the Central America on foot from the north as they followed the animal herds which provided them with their sustenance. It was not until around 5000 B.C. that we see the genesis of domesticated plant species which allowed the early settlers to establish permanent villages. These first cultivated foods include beans, squash, tomatoes, chilies, avocados, zapotes, and the all important maize. Sometime after 1000 B.C. we see the rapid emergence of a new cultural style in Guatemala with the construction of formal ceremonial and residential centers at sites along the Pacific coast. These people seem to have been Olmec or Olmec influenced judging from the style of their monumental art, reminiscent of artifacts discovered in Tabasco, Mexico and dating from as early as 1300 B.C. By 600 B.C. the human population on the Caribbean side of the isthmus was growing and it was at this time that sites such as Tikal and Uaxactun were first inhabited although it would be four hundred years before the first large temples would be built. Then around 100 B.C. we see magnificent cities

emerging from the jungle.

Society became stratified into different class: priest and royalty, artisans, temple builders, and farmers. For nearly 1000 years Maya Civilization flourished and developments in the arts and sciences rivaled those of the Old World. The ancient Maya were particularly concerned with astronomy, mathematics and the calculation of time. Powerful city-states were formed and alliances were forged between some of them in order to overpower other rival kingdoms. Then, around 900 A.D., the cities went into a period of rapid decline in an event still unexplained by science. Soon the great Mayan cities of Guatemala were reclaimed by the rain forest and only small scattered villages remained.

In 1523 Pedro de Alvarado arrived in Guatemala accompanied by 120 horsemen, 300 soldiers and 200 Mexican Indian warriors. When they arrived at Quetzalenango Valley they found the Quiché city of Xelaju abandoned. The residents had been warned and fled. Three days later the Spanish were confronted by an army of 30,000 Quiché warriors led by their great Chief Tecún Umán who appeared resplendent in a quetzal feather headdress. Despite the great disparity in numbers between the two forces Alvarado's army, armed with guns and horses was able to slaughter the Quiché and the final blow came when Chief Tecún himself was killed. That night, according to legend, innumerable quetzal birds descended upon the body of the slain Chief and kept the death watch until dawn. When they flew back into the sky their breasts had been soaked in Tecún's blood and since that day the quetzal has been red underneath.

The rest is history. For five hundred years European forces have dominated Mayan America and it is as if by a miracle that Mayan culture has persisted and thrived in the face of many adversities. Now, at the dawn of the third millennium, we see the birth of democracy and freedom of expression in Guatemala and a new era of liberty and justice for all is on the horizon. Modern Guatemala is inhabited by more than ten million souls of which perhaps half are of Mayan extraction. The other half is made up largely of Mestizos or people of mixed Spanish and Indian blood. There are also large contingents of European, Asian, African and even Middle Eastern peoples and cultures. As Guatemala enters the 21st Century it finds itself challenged by all the environmental, social, and economic problems which confront the entire planet. God has blessed Guatemala with an unusual diversity of natural and cultural richness and this muti-colored and textured fabric of Guatemalan society will provide the county with the strength and resiliency to successfully emerge as a prosperous and peaceful nation.

El Tapón, Huehuetenango Province
[OPPOSITE]

The Pan-American Highway snakes its way through the Selegua River Gorge just south of the La Mesilla boarder crossing. As you cross over from Chiapas, Mexico into Guatemala it is like crossing from one magical dream-scape into another. The scenery in Guatemala is more spectacular, the mountains seem to jut up in a more exaggerated way. It is an exotic and primitive land lined by a chain of conical volcanic cones and blanketed with mysterious cloud and pine forests.

La Mesilla Boarder Crossing
Huehuetenango Province
[BELOW]

This little boarder crossing is located on the Pan-American Highway where Chiapas, Mexico meets Guatemala.

Men of San Juan Atitán
Huehuetenango Province
[RIGHT]

There are two ways to get to the Mam Maya town of San Juan Atitán: a five hour walk through *Shangri-la* valleys and forests from the village of Todos Santos Cuchumatán or by way of an extremely rutted and frighteningly narrow track which winds up and up from the Pan-American Highway. Needless to say, very few outsiders ever visit this remote settlement.

Municipal Building, Chiantla
Huehuetenango Province
[OPPOSITE]

The Cuchumatanes Mountains
Huehuetenango Province
[RIGHT]
    Route 9N winds up and up through a series of seemingly endless switch-backs into the Cuchumatanes Mountain Range which is one of the highest areas in all Guatemala. Here the highway is often enshrouded in a cloud bank with visibility dropping to nearly zero. Ice and hail are also a frequent hazard. The views over the highlands are spectacular though and well worth the effort.

The Cinabal Plateau, Cuchumatanes
Mountains, Huehuetenango Province
[BELOW]

Cuchumatanes Mountains, Huehuetenango Province
[OPPOSITE]

Route 9N is a narrow and at times lonely secondary highway which runs from the provincial capital of Huehuetenango to the frontier outpost of Barrias. The weather can be perfectly clear one minute and a few moments later a cloud bank may move in and visibility becomes extremely restricted.

Cuchumatanes Mountains, Huehuetenango Province
[BELOW]

The Cuchumatanes Mountains are typified by pine-oak-liquidambar forests and the weather is quite cool above three thousand meters. In this photograph an underground river surfaces and creates a spectacular waterfall.

Chuy Village, Huehuetenango Province
[RIGHT]

Village men dress up in makeshift costumes and masks during the days approaching Holy Week. Here the men are busy stopping cars on the route to Todos Santos asking for a donation in the name of Judas which money, it is suspected, will be used to help fund the Easter festivities in the Village.

Cinabal Village,
Cuchumatanes Mountains, Huehuetenango Province

[OPPOSITE]

It seems that the higher the elevation and colder the weather, the brighter the colors become. In the Cuchumatanes hot pink is one of the favorite colors for clothing and the houses with all their furnishings come in all colors of the rainbow and especially bright vivid colors. The unusual esthetic sense of the local Mam and Kanjobal Maya Indians make them among the most colorful people in the world.

Paquix Village,
Cuchumatanes Mountains, Huehuetenango Province

[BELOW]

Located at approximately 3500 meters in elevation a quasi-paramo type of vegetation dominates. Here it is too cold to cultivate corn or wheat and the inhabitants dedicate themselves to sheep-herding.

Mam Indian Sheep Herders,
Cuchumatanes Mountains, Huehuetenango Province

[UPPER RIGHT]

Inhabitants of Capellania Village,
Cuchumatanes Mountains, Huehuetenango Province

[LOWER RIGHT]

Todos Santos Cuchumatán
[OPPOSITE UPPER LEFT]

Zaculeu Maya Ruins
[OPPOSITE LOWER LEFT]
   Zaculeu, located a few kilometers west of the city of
Huehuetenango, was the capital of the Mam, who were
one of the principal pre-Conquest highland tribes. The
site is thought to have been a religious and administrative
center housing the elite and includes several temples,
plazas and a ball court.

Todos Santos Cuchumatán
[OPPOSITE RIGHT]
   An itinerant herb salesman hawks his wares at the
village plaza. Coyote oil for arthritis, herbs for stomach
aches, roots for lack of energy and ground rattlesnake
for cancer.

Maximon of Todos Santos Cuchumatán
[RIGHT]

Sacred Corn Kernels
[BELOW]
   Corn is the sacred food of the Maya and comes in the
four holy colors of white, red, yellow and black. Every
aspect of the cultivation of corn is carried out with
ceremony and special care. The blessing of the fields
by the local Mayan Priest, the planting, the tending of
the young plants, the harvest, and the preparation of
tortillas, tamales, chuchitos, atól, and the fermented
corn brew called boc all attended to with the utmost
care and reverence as a sacred ritual.

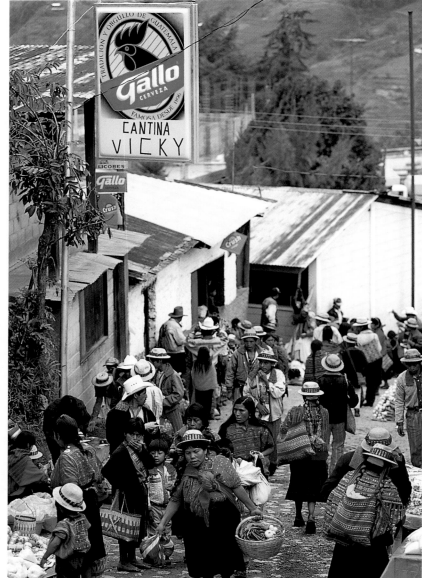

Todos Santos Cuchumatán

[OPPOSITE LEFT]

Friendly Children greet visitors from the four corners of the world with their charming and playful spirits.

Todos Santos Cuchumatán

[OPPOSITE RIGHT]

Main Street during Market Day.

San Juan Atitán

[BELOW AND RIGHT]

San Juan Atitán is a four hour walk from the Mam population center of Todos Santos Cuchumatán and requires the sturdy hiker to climb up the dirt path along a series of endless switchbacks leading to the ridge and then down into a beautiful isolated valley where San Juan Atitán sits perched on a steep slope. The main market days are Monday and Thursday when the normally sleepy town becomes a bustling center of activity. Market day is much more than an occasion to conduct business. It is a time for meeting friends, treating the children to an ice cream, and maybe even catching a movie. Rambo, Bruce Lee and Chuck Noris always seem to draw the biggest crowds! The distinctive costumes worn by the Mam make Market Day a dazzling spectacle.

San Juan Atitán, Huehuetenango Province
[LEFT]

San Rafael Petzal, Huehuetenango Province
[BELOW]

Ixtahuacán, Huehuetenango Province
[OPPOSITE UPPER LEFT]
  Mam Indian workers at the local tungsten mine prepare do descend into the depths of the Earth.

San Juan Atitán, Huehuetenango Province
[OPPOSITE UPPER RIGHT, LOWER MIDDLE AND LOWER RIGHT]

San Mateo Ixtatán, Huehuetenango Province
[OPPOSITE LOWER LEFT]
  The distinctive women's costume of San Mateo Ixtatán is made of thick hand-woven material

San Pedro Necta, *Huehuetenango Province*
[OPPOSITE LEFT]
   Market Day.

San Pedro Necta, *Huehuetenango Province*
[OPPOSITE RIGHT]
   Spectacular costume and ornamentation evoke the vision of a Mayan Princess. The traditional textiles of the inhabitants of Huehuetenango Province are among the brightest and most colorful of the entire Mayan World.

Ixtahuacán, *Huehuetenango Province*
[RIGHT]
   After the daily Mass.

Colotenango, *Huehuetenango Province*
[MIDDLE]
   Market Day.

Ixtahuacán, *Huehuetanango Province*
[BELOW]
   Market Day.

Santa Maria Volcano Towers
Over the Quetzaltenango Valley, Quetzaltenango Province
[OPPOSITE]

The Village Laundry, Zunil, Quetzaltenango Province
[BELOW]

San Francisco El Alto, Totonicapán Province
[RIGHT]
   The Friday market at San Francisco El Alto is the largest traditional market in the country where traders from all over Guatemala converge to sell everything from pigs and turkeys to radios, cooking utensils, and food of every variety. Selling begins as early as 4 AM and shortly after dawn the central plaza located, adjacent to the church, is buzzing with activity.

Zunil, Quetzaltenango Province
[LEFT]
The traditional women's costume of Zunil is of unequaled beauty.

Zunil, Quetzaltenango Province
[RIGHT]
Tending the garden.

San Andrés Xecul, Quetzaltenango Province
[OPPOSITE LEFT]
Everywhere you look in Highland Guatemala the visitor is greeted with the gay and colorful Mayan esthetic. The brighter the colors the better and it seems that just about anything goes....but, somehow, it all seems to work. Here at the Catholic Church at San Andrés Xecul Mayan motifs blend with traditional Christian images to create a uniquely Guatemalan house of worship.

Traditional Women's Costume, Quetzaltenango
[OPPOSITE RIGHT]

**Quetzaltenango Valley
as seen from the Pan-American Highway.**
[LEFT]

Zunil, Quetzaltenango Province
[OPPOSITE UPPER LEFT]
   Fresh news and gossip are exchanged by women during Market day.

Zunil, Quetzaltenango Province
[OPPOSITE UPPER MIDDLE]
   A women returns home from the market. She carries on her head one of the mornings acquisitions: a stone mortar that is used to grind corn and other foods.

San Pedro Necta, Huehuetenango Province
[OPPOSITE UPPER RIGHT]
   Market Day.

**San Martin Chile Verde
Quetzaltenango Province**
[OPPOSITE LOWER LEFT]

Zunil,Quetzaltenango Province
[OPPOSITE LOWER RIGHT]
   The Indoor Market.

Downtown Quetzaltenango
[OPPOSITE LEFT]
Pasaje Enriquez.

Downtown Quetzaltenango
[OPPOSITE UPPER RIGHT]

Downtown Quetzaltenango
[OPPOSITE LOWER RIGHT]
Parque Centro America. Greek style columns and monuments distinguish Quetzaltenango's Central Park.

Plaza Tecún Umán, Quetzaltenango
[UPPER MIDDLE]
Tecún Umán is considered one of Guatemala's National Heros. It was the Great Chief Tecún Umán who faced the Spanish invaders headed by Pedro de Alvarado on the battlefield of Xelahu. In a fierce battle Alvarado killed Tecún. That night countless numbers of quetzal birds rested upon the body of the slain leader keeping a death watch. Since that day the quetzal has been red underneath. This sculpture is by Guatemalan artist Rodolfo Galeotti Torres.

Sierra Panimaquin, Quetzaltenango Province
[UPPER RIGHT]
Superb camping at the edge of the cloud forest can be found at several of the public hot springs located along the flanks of the Sierra Panimaquin.

Quetzaltenango City
[LOWER RIGHT]
The second largest city in Guatemala.

Zunil, Quetzaltenango Province
[BELOW]

Nahualá, Sololá Province
[LEFT]

Los Riscos de Momostenango
Totonicapán Province
[OPPOSITE UPPER LEFT]

The "riscos" are a series of strange looking sandstone pillars located a short walk from the town center. The name "Momostenango" means "the place of the altars" and has been special sacred site for the Maya since pre-Colombian times. It is here where the ceremony of the *Guaxaquib Batz* is performed that begins the new year according to the Mayan calender which is based upon the ancient 260 day *Tzolkin* year.

Pacific Ring of Fire
[OPPOSITE BELOW]

The entire coast of Central America is lined with a series of Volcanos which make up a section of the so called Pacific Ring of Fire which circumscribes the entire Pacific Ocean. Guatemala is an extremely active tectonic area and usually three volcanos can be seen spewing up ash and lava.

The Central Highlands, Sololá Province
[OPPOSITE UPPER RIGHT]

The Meat Market, Zunil
[BELOW]

Nebaj, Quiché Province
[OPPOSITE]
  Market Day.

Chichicastenango, Quiché Province
[UPPER LEFT]
  Sunday Market.

Nebaj Village, Quiché Province
[RIGHT]

Route 9S, Quetzaltenango Province
[BELOW]
  The main route which runs between the provincial capital of Quetzaltenango and the Pacific port of Champerico.

Lake Atitlán National Park
Sololá Province
[OPPOSITE]

The villages of San Pedro and San Juan are nestled at the foot of enormous San Pedro Volcano. The lake measures 18 kilometers long by 12 kilometers at its widest point. It is at least half a kilometer deep. The elevation at the shore is 1562 meters providing spring-like weather the year round.

Florinda and Rosita from Santa Catarina Palopó
[RIGHT]

Little Street Vendor, Panajachel
[UPPER MIDDLE]

The Comedor, Chichicastenango
[BELOW]

Small rustic open kitchens are always in abundance at the local markets. Nutritious meals of tortillas, beans, and chicken stew are served.

View of Lake Atitlán from Tierra Blanca
[OPPOSITE]

Dressed for Action, Panajachel
[UPPER MIDDLE]

Lake Atitlán: Cerro de Oro and
San Pedro Volcano
[UPPER RIGHT]

Fine Restaurants in Panajachel
[LOWER LEFT]

President William Jefferson Clinton
Makes a Surprise Appearance During
the Annual Convite Celebrations on Calle
Santander in Panajachel
[LOWER RIGHT]

Boys of San Lucas Toliman Dressed in Special Costumes for the Easter Celebration
[OPPOSITE]

The Santo Thomas Church at Chichicastenango, El Quiché Province
[UPPER MIDDLE]

Childern of Santa Cruz La Laguna Enjoy a Mauually Operated Ferris Wheel.
[LOWER MIDDLE]

Corina and Grandma from Barrio Jucanya, Province of Sololá
[RIGHT]

Solumn Procession of Easter Santiago Atitlán
[LOWER LEFT]

Pacaya Volcano Event, 1987
[RIGHT]

The largest spectacular eruption of Guatemala's most active volcano occurred in 1987. As it happens, I had been watching Pacaya for several weeks and had noticed the eruptions were getting better and better. One January day I decided to drive to the upper slopes of the cone to try and get some photos for my archives. I was accompanied by my friend Maxy Shitsumi who borrowed a vehicle from her aunt. We drove right up to the lava fields on a little dirt track out from the village of San Vicente Pacaya and from this vantage point we had a spectacular view of the cone. We arrived at mid-afternoon and the fiery lava was spewing at least a hundred meters up. The site was impressive and I set up my equipment with the idea of waiting until dusk when the conditions would be ideal for photos. As the afternoon wore on the volcano increased in activity and the eruptions became steadily higher and more frequent. By five o'clock the emissions were taking place every twenty to thirty seconds and were reaching several hundred meters in height. It was getting exciting! As dusk approached things were becoming increasingly wild. The eruptions were getting closer together and the noise of the periodic deafening explosions were causing us to feel more than a little nervous.

By now a steady stream of vehicles were racing by as the terrified residents from the little town of Caracol were evacuated. I continued to take photos. Maxy was loosing her cool, pleading that we should get out of there as I procrastinated hoping to get a super shot. Right at nightfall all hell broke loose. Pacaya started looking like a roman candle as the lava shot more than one kilometer into the sky and a deep, ultra-low frequency roar came from all directions. It was getting *way* too hot and Maxy ran for the car, threw it into reverse and got the vehicle hopelessly stuck in the powder-fine ash at the side of the road! Now we had no way to escape. Fear gripped my heart. We were going to have to abandon everything and run for our lives. Just then a last straggler from Caracol drove past. Seeing our plight, he helped pull our car out. Saved! We drove full speed down and down the switch-backs with the ominous orange glow filling the sky behind us. One of my fondest memories is of the cold beers we drank that night after almost being *carbonized!*

Event at Pacaya Volcano, February, 2000
[OPPOSITE ,BELOW AND RIGHT]

We were all exhausted after a long day exploring the coast near Retalhuleu and I was driving the Trooper as friends Joe, Mayer and Maya Jean slept. I noticed an orange glow way off in the sky. Was it possible that I was seeing Pacaya erupting nearly 100 kilometers away? I started to get excited. Sure enough, more than an hour later as we left the coastal town of Esquintla we caught an amazing view of the unusual fiery display. It was late, but I convinced my companions that we should drive up closer. "I know a good spot where I got some great photos years ago" I said. All agreed and Joe took the wheel. Up and up we drove. From the area around San Vicente Pacaya the view was superb (photo at right). We continued on toward the lava field. We expected to meet other volcano watchers up there but the place was abandoned. The eruptions were getting higher and the full moon was out. We were all elated. Joe wanted to continue to drive around Pacaya. I warned that I had no knowledge of road conditions beyond where we were but Joe insisted so we drove on. As we passed through the little village of Caracol there was not a soul in sight. I warned again that I did not think it was safe to continue, that the road went nowhere with no outlet, but Joe insisted saying that he thought we could drive all the way around the cone. As we descended south of Caracol the road conditions became worse and worse and soon it was beginning to look grim as the steep narrow track began to disappear in the soft ash. The road down to hell! I was having deja vu all over again and starting to feel nervous. The eruptions were getting stronger and now we were stuck on the south side of the cone; historically the worst place to be; where most of Pacayas victims had lost their lives. It was obvious to me that the slope we were stuck on had been recently blanketed with thick ash. The fumes from the volcano were beginning to make me feel queasy. "Isn't that river of lava starting to head our way?" stuttered Maya Jean? Mayer was not looking pleased. Now we had to think how to survive. Joe tried his cell phone praying for a bailout. Dead! He went back up the track to look for help. The rest of us were getting ready to abandon the vehicle and make our way down the slope the best we could. As fate would have it Joe returned half an hour later with two natives who had not abandoned Caracol. There was a way out! they told us and proceeded to guide us down an endless series or gullies and invisible trails until we finally did get out. It had been one beautiful, scary, intense night!

Esquipulas, Chiquimula Province
[LEFT AND OPPOSITE]

We returned to breakfast and afterwards set out to visit the only object of interest, the great church of the pilgrimage, the Holy Place of Central America. Every year on the fifteenth of January, pilgrims visit it, even from Peru and Mexico; the latter being a journey not exceeded in hardship by the pilgrimage to Mecca. As in the east "it is not forbidden to trade during the pilgrimage," and when there are no wars to make the roads unsafe eighty thousand people have assembled among the mountains to barter and pay homage to "our Lord of Esquipulas."
        -John Lloyd Stepherns, 1841.

More than a century after the above commentary was written by the intrepid British traveler, Esquipulas remains the most important sacred site in Mesoamerica and pilgrims from all over come to vernerate the figure of the Black Christ. The beautiful Basilica is maintained by an international contingent of Benadictine Monks. The history of the pilgrimage probably goes back to the days before the Conquest when the valley was under the control of Chief Esquipulas. The famous image of Christ was carved by famed colonial sculptor Quirio Cataño and installed in the church in 1595.

Special Hats Symbolize the Pilgrimage to Esquipulas
[UPPER LEFT]

Pope John Paul's Historic Visit to Esquipulas in 1997
[LOWER LEFT]

A Pilgrim Awaits Her Special Blessing
[BELOW]

Sprinkling With Holy Water
[OPPOSITE UPPER LEFT AND MIDDLE]

Tradition requires that the pilgrim wait in line to receive a special blessing and be sprinkled with Holy Water. Just about anything can and is blessed from paintings of the Black Christ to babies, to damaged limbs. It has become a tradition also for drivers to come and have their vehicles blessed. This is especially true for bus and truck drivers.

Inside the Basilica of Esquipulas
[OPPOSITE LOWER LEFT AND RIGHT]

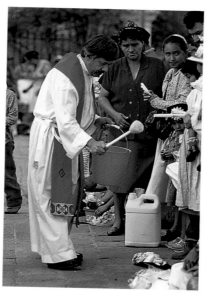

The Resplendent Quetzal
[OPPOSITE LEFT]

The resplendent quetzal is the largest and most spectacular member of the pan-tropical *Trogon* family of birds. Quetzals live exclusively in the high cloud forest which exists along the Pacific slope of the chain of volcanos as well in the upper highlands and the Vera Paz provinces.

Cloud Forest, Alta Verapaz Province
[OPPOSITE RIGHT]

Cloud Forest, Sierra de las Minas Biosphere Reserve
[BELOW]

El Salto Falls, Alta Verapaz Province
[RIGHT]

Tzalamilá, Alta Verapaz
[OPPOSITE, UPPER LEFT AND UPPER RIGHT]

Every year during the annual festival in honor of the villages Patron Saint the men of Tzalamilá dress up in special ceremonial costumes to perform the Dance of the Conquest, the Deer Dance and other choreographed theatrical presentations depicting important historical events, supernatural entities, and Mayan cosmovision.

Kek'chi Ceremonial Dance Mask Depicting Pedro de Alvarado
[UPPER MIDDLE]

Ox Cart, Coban, Alta Verapaz Province
[OPPOSITE UPPER RIGHT AND LEFT]

Once the main vehicle used to transport cargo, ox carts are still in use today in the villages of Verapaz.

Nobel Prize Winner and Indigenous Leader Rigoberta Menchú Tum
[BELOW]

The Maximón Temple of San Andrés Itzapa, Chimaltenango Province
[OPPOSITE]

It would be impossible to find a single village in all of highland Guatemala where the presence of Maximon is not felt. Maximon's influence extends beyond Guatemala and shrines for his adoration can be found in Mexico, Honduras, Belize, and even in New York City. But who is this Maximon? That is not an easy question to answer and it depends on who you ask. Maximon is the Patron Saint of Mayan Sorcerers, he is an indigenous deity, he intercedes on behalf of those who believe in him and helps those who are in need. In Guatemala there are three well known Maximon temples where tourists are allowed to visit: San Andrés Itzapa is the largest temple; then there is Maximon of Zunil and also Maximon of Santiago Atitlán at Lake Atitlán. But the truth is every town has its own Maximon shrine...some small and humble, some quite large and elaborate.

Maximón Temple in Sololá Province
[UPPER AND LOWER RIGHT]

This unusual underground temple is presided over by a highly respected Mayan Priest who is expert in performing the rituals and incantations necessary to insure a positive outcome whether the problem is physical illness, bad luck, trouble in marriage, or the curse of an evil shaman. In this temple a trio of Maximon figures adorns the alter showing the wide variety of Maximon images. On the alter Jesus Christ and other Christian Saints are also prominent.

Maximón of San Antonio Aquas Calientes, Sacatepéquez Province and Maximón of San Lucas Tolimán, Sololá Province
[LOWER LEFT AND LOWER MIDDLE]

Maximón of Todos Saints Cuchumatán
[LEFT]

Maximón in a Private Home Shrine
[UPPER RIGHT]

Trio of Maximón Figures
[LOWER RIGHT]

Shamanic Temple In Retalhuleu Province
[OPPOSITE]

   Mr. Mayer Schames, who describes himself as the son of a Jewish Rabbi-Shaman, has traveled from Los Angeles, California to be present at a special *Costumbre* or spiritual service where a respected Mayan Priest and Shaman uses a variety of incantations and rituals to invoke the supernatural forces and create a healing vibration. The Priest was also able to comment on the condition and future of Mr. Schames' family in the United States as will as predict that the all the visitors present could expect to experience safe and healthy lives for the foreseeable future.

Giant Spirit Kites Sacatepéquez Province

[THIS PAGE AND OPPOSITE]

Every year on the first of November several villages in Sacatepéquez Province fly the famous giant kites. This occasion is known as the Day of The Dead and friends and family members of the deceased visit the cemeteries and adorn the tombs with flowers and bright colored ornaments and wreaths. Construction of the kites, which may measure more then ten meters in diameter, is begun months before and every year new themes and styles appear. It seems that anything goes and images on the kites range from famous movie personalties to Catholic Saints to promotional material for social change and solidarity.

The National Palace
[UPPER LEFT]

Construction of the National Palace began in 1939 under the auspices of then president Jorge Ubico and completed a year before he was ousted in 1944. The Palace is the most impressive of any in Central America in incorporates many fine created by local artisans.

The National Theater
[LOWER LEFT]

Built at the top of San José Fortress, the National Theater is one of the most unusual and prominent buildings of Guatemala City.

The Palace Honor Guard
[OPPOSITE UPPER LEFT]

Kids of the Corleto Clan Residents of Guatemala City
[OPPOSITE UPPER MIDDLE]

Guatemala City Barrio
[OPPOSITE UPPER RIGHT]

Sixth Avenue, Downtown Guatemala City
[OPPOSITE LOWER LEFT]

The National Post Office Building Downtown Guatemala City
[OPPOSITE LOWER RIGHT]

Easter Procession and the Metropolitan Cathedral
[LEFT]

Construction of the Cathedral was begun in 1782 and was not completed until 1868. Its facade combines elements of Baroque and Neoclassical styles.

Museum of Archaeology and Ethnology
[BELOW]

A sculpture of indigenous hero Tecun Uman at the entrance of the Museum.

Dusk over Guatemala City
[OPPOSITE ABOVE]

Zone 10, Guatemala City
[OPPOSITE LOWER LEFT]

Known as "La Zona Viva" Zone 10 is the most upscale and modern sector of the city where fine restaurants, hotels and shops are in abundance.

Areal View of Guatemala City
[OPPOSITE LOWER RIGHT]

Calle del Arco, Antigua Guatemala
[OPPOSITE UPPER LEFT]

The Arch of Santa Catalina is all that is left of the original convent which was established here in 1609. By 1697 the convent housed more than 100 nuns and the arch was built so that the women could cross the street which divided the two halves of the convent without having to have contact with the mundane world outside,

La Merced Church, Antigua Guatemala
[OPPOSITE UPPER RIGHT]

This church was established by the Mercedarian Brothers and includes one of the most intricate and impressive facades in the city.

Easter Processions, Antigua Guatemala
[OPPOSITE LOWER LEFT , RIGHT AND BELOW]

Agua Volcano Towers over the City of Antigua as Seen from Cerro de la Cruz
[RIGHT]

World Famous Antigua Coffee
[UPPER LEFT]

The region around Antigua Guatemala is one of the countries most important coffee growing areas. The rich volcanic soils and cool temperate climate create the ideal conditions necessary for producing the worlds finest coffee. The harvest of the ripe red "beans" takes place in the spring during the early months of the dry season.

El Desayuno Típico
[LOWER LEFT]

El Desayuno Tipico is the special Guatemalan breakfast. Always included are eggs prepared in a variety of styles: here fried sunny side up with a tomato sauce on top, *frijoles* or black beans which may be served re-fried as seen here or *parados*, which means whole, fried plantains, fresh farmer's cheese, fresh fruit in season, hand made tortillas (Guatemalans abhor machine made tortillas) and a cup of the worlds finest coffee.

La Marimba: The Traditional Music of Guatemala
[BELOW]

Fine Guatemalan Textiles
[OPPOSITE]

The staff of world famous NIM PO'T Centro de Textiles Tradicionales and Retail Textile Museum model some of the establishments exquisite Mayan fabrics which represent styles from all around the country..

Dance of the Twenty-four Devils
Ciudad Vieja, Sacatepéquez Province
[OPPOSITE LEFT]

Holy Week Procession, Antigua Guaemala
[OPPOSITE RIGHT]

Church at San Felipe Sacatepéquez
Province
[UPPER LEFT]

La Posada del Angel, Antigua Guaemala
[UPPER AND LOWER RIGHT]

Agua Volcano Towers Over the Calle de
Las Campanas
[BELOW]

Hand Made Mayan Fabrics at Nim Po't Center for Traditional Textiles
[THIS PAGE AND OPPOSITE]

Mayan cultural traditions are alive and well in Guatemala and this is especially true when it comes to the weaving of cloth. It is not uncommon to see three or four generations of women sitting outside their house all busy weaving on their back-strap looms. It would be cheaper and easier for them to buy clothing and fabric in a store but there is something mystical and magical about patiently weaving cloth and making your own clothing with its distinctive and very personal style and design.The vibrant weaving tradition of the Maya and the unique costumes with which they adorn themselves give them a powerful sense of identity and pride which is largely lost in the modern world of machine made clothing. As can be seen on these pages, the Maya love bright colors and striking designs and this reflects the inner world of their imagination. Mayan people tend to be quiet, shy and very polite but the wild colors and motifs which they choose show that the Maya are really extremely fun loving, happy, and imaginative people with a tremendous sense of humor, full with the joy of living.

Carnival at Mazatenango, Suchitepéquez Province
[THIS PAGE, OPPOSITE AND FOLLOWING TWO PAGES]

   The tradition of Carnival in Mazatenango goes back more than 100 years. The festival goes on for more than a week during with there are numerous processions, dances, street parties and special events. March groups from around the province of Suchitepéquez participate and many months of work go into the preparation of the costumes and floats. Since the people of this province are not particularly wealthy every bit of imagination is used to come up with new and exciting carnival outfits with the idea of winning the competition of best in category. Beauty queens from all over the country participate in the processions and events. Extraordinarily, the *Mazate* carnival, which is one of the largest and most impressive and fun festivals in all Guatemala has yet to be discovered by the tourist industry and is attended almost exclusively by local inhabitants.

Puerto Champerico, Retalhuleu Province
[UPPER LEFT]
  Black volcanic sand beaches are a unique feature of the Pacific Coast of Guatemala.

Puerto Champerico, Retalhuleu Province
[LOWER LEFT]
  Young dock workers

Puerto Quetzal, Esquintla Province
[LOWER RIGHT]

National Police Station, Retalhuleu
[OPPOSITE UPPER LEFT]

The Train, Retalhleu
[OPPOSITE LOWER LEFT]

Train Station, Mazatenango
[OPPOSITE RIGHT]

Sugar Cane Field
[OPPOSITE UPPER LEFT]
   Sugar production is one of the most important industries of the southern coastal plain. Here we see a recently planted cane field in Esquintla Province.

The Sugar Harvest
[OPPOSITE LOWER LEFT]

Processing the Sugar Cane Juice
[OPPOSITE RIGHT]

Extracting the Sugar Cane Juice from the Cane Pulp
[LOWER LEFT]

Entrance to a Large Sugar Plantation, Suchitepéquez Province
[UPPER RIGHT]

Processed Sugar Being Shipped Overseas, Puerto Quetzal, Esquintla Province
[LOWER RIGHT]

Monterrico Nature Reserve, Santa Rosa Province
[OPPOSITE UPPER LEFT]

The Biotopo Nature Reserve at Monterrico is one of most beautiful and pristine estuarine habitats remaining along the south coast of Guatemala. It is designated as a multiple use area and here local a local fisherman tries his luck with the hope of netting some snook or *mojarra* fish.

Monterrico Nature Reserve, Santa Rosa Province
[OPPOSITE LOWER LEFT AND RIGHT]

The inner lagoons at Monterrico provide critical habitat to local and migratory bird species.

Ceiba Flower
[UPPER LEFT]

The Ceiba, or kapok tree is the sacred tree of the Maya and is abundant along the south coast of Guatemala.

Abaj Takalik Maya Ruins, Retalhuleu Province
[UPPER RIGHT]

The people who built this ceremonial center predated the Maya and are thought to have been related to the Olmec culture which flourished along the gulf coast of Mexico around 400 BC.

Hobie Cat Regatta at Puerto Quetzal, Esquintla Province
[BELOW]

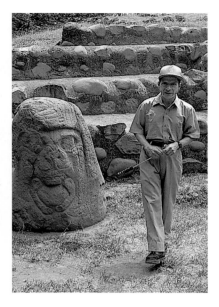

The Rio Dulce

[THIS PAGE AND OPPOSITE]

One of the largest and most magnificent rivers in Central America, the Rio Dulce, which means sweet river, is a favorite hang out for the international yachting crowd. The river provides a safe anchorage during the hurricane season and is an ideal spot for a captain to leave his vessel for a few weeks and explore the highlands of Guatemala. Rio Dulce is also the weekend mecca for thousands of residents from Guatemala City who are dying for a little sun and fresh air. The river and the adjacent Lake Izabal are a true paradise for fishermen, bird watchers, naturalists and sun worshipers.

Quiriguá Maya Ruins, Izabal Province
[LEFT AND BELOW]

Of one thing there is no doubt; a large city once stood there; its name is lost, its history unknown; and no account of its existence has ever before been published. For centuries it has lain as completely buried as if covered with the lava of Vesuvius. Every traveler from Yzabal to Guatemala has passed within three hours of it; we ourselves had done the same; and yet there it lay, like the rock-built city of Edom, unvisited, unsought, and utterly unknown.

John Lloyd Stephens, 1841

The first evidence of human habitation on this site dates to 250 BC when migrants from the north, probably from the Yucatán peninsula, arrived and established themselves. During the Classic Period the Quiriguá became a busy center and its location along the Motagua River trade route along with the fact that the surrounding mountains are rich with jade added to the cities importance. It is here where some of the largest and most ornate stela and monumental carvings of the entire Mayan world are found.

Finca Ixobel, El Petén Province
[OPPOSITE UPPER AND LOWER LEFT]

For several decades now Finca Ixobel has been one of the premier eco-tourism destinations along the Ruta Maya. Nestled in the foothills of the Maya Mountains and blessed with an ideal climate, Ixobel is an ideal base from which to explore the pristine forests of El Peten Province.

Forty-five Minute Cave, El Petén Province
[OPPOSITE RIGHT]

Finca Ixobel, El Peten Province
[UPPER LEFT]

Scarlet Macaw
[LOWER LEFT]

Christmas at the Guatemalan Air Force Base Santa Elena, El Petén Province
[LOWER LEFT , RIGHT AND BELOW]

Co-op Technica Agropecuaria, Along the Usumacinta River El Petén Province
[OPPOSITE UPPER LEFT]

The Chile Harvest, Usumacinta River, El Petén Province
[OPPOSITE LOWER LEFT]

Lake Petén Itzá, El Petén Province
[OPPOSITE RIGHT]

Pyramid of the Masks, Tikal National Park, El Petén Province
[OPPOSITE LEFT]

A group of Kek'chi Maya Indians from a nearby village visit the ruins to conduct special rituals designed to insure a good corn crop and the abundant rains which their lives depend upon.

Detail of Stela 31, Erected in AD 445, Tikal National Park
[OPPOSITE UPPER RIGHT]

The North Acropolis, Tikal National Park
[OPPOSITE LOWER RIGHT]

One the surface the North Acropolis is comprised of a complex of large pyramids and palaces but buried underneath have been discovered the vestiges of more than 100 structures including some of the oldest found at Tikal dating as early as 600 BC.

Pyramid of the Giant Jaguar, Tikal National Park
[BELOW]

The Pyramid of the Giant Jaguar rises 45 meters above the Great Plaza and faces west toward the setting sun, considered by the ancient Maya to be the portal to the Underworld.

Mayan Shaman Perform Sacred Rituals, Tikal National Park
[RIGHT]

Tikal National Park and Uaxactún Maya Ruins
[FOLLOWING TWO PAGES]

Exploring the Maya Biosphere Reserve, El Petén Province
[OPPOSITE]

Comprised of more than one million hectares the Maya Biosphere Reserve is unquestionably the largest and one of the most important nature reserves in Guatemala and is certainly of great significance on a planetary level. Made up primarily of rain forest the reserve provide critical habitat for countless plant and animal species including many threatened migratory bird species.

Butterfly, Maya Biosphere Reserve
[BELOW]

Morpho Butterfly, Maya Biosphere Reserve
[RIGHT]

Shortly after emerging from its chrysalis the butterfly must rest for several hours to dry its wings and prepare for flight. The blue morpho is beautifully iridescent and flashes brightly as it flits around the forest understory.

Wildflower
[OPPOSITE LEFT]

Moth
[OPPOSITE UPPER RIGHT]

Caterpillar
[OPPOSITE LOWER RIGHT]

Terrestrial Orchid
[LOWER LEFT]

Tapir
[UPPER RIGHT]

The Tapir is the largest terrestrial herbivore in Central America. They are gentle and shy and love to forage the tender grasses that grow along river banks.

Millipede
[LOWER RIGHT]

Not to be confused with the aggressive and poisonous centipede, the millipede is a peaceful forager of the forest floor and is completely harmless.

Dragonfly
[OPPOSITE LEFT]

Orchid
[OPPOSITE UPPER RIGHT]

Miniature Orchid
[OPPOSITE LOWER RIGHT]

Wildflower
[BELOW]

Wildflower
[UPPER LEFT]

Wildflower
[UPPER RIGHT]

Butterfly
[LOWER RIGHT]

I never intended on coming to Guatemala. I was in a pre-med program at the University of San Francisco in 1973 and when summer vacation arrived I hopped on my Honda 350 and headed south with no planned destination. I just wanted to travel and explore a new world. When I arrived at Lake Atitlán I found the atmosphere so beautiful, inspiring and relaxing that I decided to stay for several months. I enjoyed interacting with the Mayan people even though verbal communication was very limited. And dinners at Mama's in Jucanya were always a great time with great company. I toured the back roads of Petén, Alta Verapaz and Huehuetenango and was continuously amazed by the sublime profusion and diversity of life to be found in these tropical environments. This was a time when very few tourists were ever to be found along the back roads of Guatemala. I found the native Mayan and campesino inhabitants to be unusually friendly and hospitable and many times I set up my little tent beside a humble jungle shack. Almost invariably I would be invited to share a meal with my hosts no matter how poor they might have been. Of course, that would give me a chance to share some exotic food item with them: like a tin of tuna fish or some peanut butter. That always brought great joy to my new friends. I felt like an extra terrestrial visiting a newly discovered planet.

Renowned Belizean jungle guide David "Bantam" Simpson with author Thor "Bushman Ollie" Janson

The time came for me to continue my travels and I drove south to Panama where I got a job as chief navigator aboard a 64 foot sailboat headed for Australia. During the next year's travels around the world I kept remembering the happy times I had had in Guatemala and in late 1974 decided to return. For the next year I lived with a Cak'Chiquel family on the shores of Lake Atitlán, exploring the forests and learning to speak Spanish.

In 1976 I met don Edgar Bauer who, at the time, was the official in charge of Lake Atitlán National Park. I explained to him that I wanted to get involved with wildlife conservation and Edgar told me to go see the Guatemala's pioneer conservationist Dr. Mario Dary Rivera. It was also don Edgar who informed me than the manatee of Lake Izabal were a species in need of protection. I soon became good friends with Mario Dary and he invited me to join the Faculty of the School of Biology at San Carlos University which he headed. During the next five years Dary gave me invaluable support as I studied the endangered sea cows and developed programs of environmental education for the country. Then in 1981 Dary was assassinated and our work together was ended.

In 1982, as I was exploring the coast of Belize in my little sailboat, the idea came to me to form my own ecology organization and thus was born Defensores de la Naturaleza which I established in Guatemala in 1983. For the next five years I directed the development of Defensores activities which began with a wide scale education campaign followed by an innovative private reserve project. At present I direct the Embajada del Reino Natural which is an organization dedicated to the preservation of wilderness and to promoting reforestation efforts worldwide.

I wish to express special thanks to my publisher Señor Jesus Chico for supporting my work over the past decade and for making this book possible.

I give thanks to Abba Jah, without Him there would be no life.
Thy will be done on Earth as it is in Heaven.
This book is dedicated to all those who love Truth.
"ONLY THE IMPOSSIBLE ALWAYS HAPPENS" -Buckminster Fuller
Produced by the Watusi Alí Experience.
Final Production by Jorge "Night Breed" Paz.

Front Cover: Pacya Volcano, February 2000.
Front Cover Flap: Tikal
Back Cover Flap:Matilde

Editorial Artemis Edinter
12 Calle, 10-55, Zona 1
Guatemala City, Guatemala, Central America
e-mail: artemisedint@gold.guate.net   FAX: 502-238-0866
Thor Janson e-mail: brotherijah@hotmail.com